Do you wish you could hit the ball harder?

Do you hit the ball late?

Do you have trouble hitting the ball where you want to?

Do you have tennis elbow?

Do you get "the" elbow?

Are you a B player who would like to be an A? Or a C who would like to be a B?

Do you have trouble winning tie-breakers?

Is your toss all over the place?

Are you afraid of the net?

Does it make you nervous to compete?

Are you exhausted after playing for only an hour?

If any of these questions apply to you, relax—there's help ahead. Inside this book are the answers to your nagging tennis problems, and ways to show you how to enjoy your game and win.

SALLY MOORE HUSS was born in Bakersfield, California, and spent her early years concentrating on tennis—playing, training, and traveling. Her hard work was to later make her a U.S. clay court champion, a Wimbledon semi-finalist, and a Virginia Slims touring pro. She also represented the United States twice on the Wightman Cup Team, and in 1975 her tournament record won her a ranking of thirtieth among women players internationally. In the early seventies, Ms. Huss decided to teach tennis professionally in Beverly Hills, Malibu, and Palm Springs, introducing special techniques to help players move freely and play powerfully. Her roster of students reads like a Hollywood Who's Who, including such names as Merv Griffin, Joel Grey, Jill St. John, Samuel Goldwyn, Jr., Barbra Streisand, Helen Reddy, and many more.

Ms. Huss has many talents. She is a partner and design consultant for the Michele Palmer line of quality tennis clothes and draws tennis cartoons for various magazines (she was an art major at the University of Southern California and Occidental College), most notably *World Tennis.*

Currently she teaches and lives in Aspen, Colorado, with her husband, Marvin, and their baby son Michael.

How to Play
Power Tennis
with Ease

How to Play

written and illustrated

Harcourt Brace Jovanovich

Power Tennis

with Ease

by Sally Moore Huss

New York and London

Requests for permission to make copies of any part of the work
should be mailed to:
Permissions, Harcourt Brace Jovanovich, Inc.,
757 Third Avenue, New York, New York 10017

Printed in the United States of America

Library of Congress Cataloging in Publication Data

Huss, Sally Moore.
How to play power tennis with ease.
1. Tennis. I. Title.
GV995.H86   796.34'22   78–20569
ISBN 0–15–236836–1

First edition

B C D E

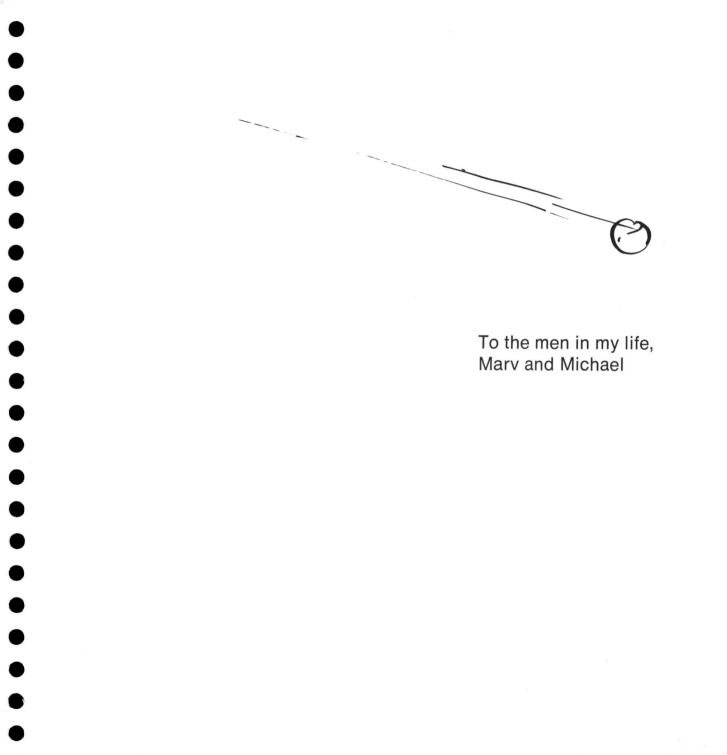

To the men in my life,
Marv and Michael

Contents

Where does real power come from in playing tennis? It does *not* come from muscle force and mechanical action. It comes from swinging the head of the racket freely through space. This swinging produces natural timing, rhythm, and grace. Muscle force and mechanical action produce a tense, pushy, restrictive motion and may lead to physical problems such as tennis elbow. It is also hard work. If instead the head of the racket is swung freely, power surges from it and into the oncoming ball.

In the hammer throw, power is generated by swinging a heavy weight centrifugally on a chain, which is then released. In golf, the head of the club is swung as if on a tether, and the rest of the body follows as the force of the club head moves through the ball. The same principle applies in playing tennis, but not everyone knows it or knows how to do it.

Most people are taught to play tennis mechanically with strict forms and strict patterns of strategy and play. I was taught this way and played fairly well. I had won both the Wimbledon and U.S. Junior Championships, reached the semifinals at Wimbledon one year, and was twice a member of the U.S. Wightman Cup team. But it wasn't any fun. It was work. Many times I had to start from scratch to regroove my mechanically learned forehand after losing the line of it. I worried, and I discovered most other players experienced similar problems because they had learned their strokes in this unnatural way too. Finally I decided to quit.

Years later after working with a teacher in free-dance movement and playing only relaxed, social tennis, I began to use the head of the racket to play in a most unusual way. I began to swing the racket freely and with very little effort sent back the balls with amazing speed and accuracy. It was a great feeling. I loved playing and won consistently.

Suddenly I wanted to teach! I wanted to share what I had found from experience to be true and effective—tennis that was *easy* to learn: relaxed, graceful, and yet *powerful.* (Prior to this I would never have considered the idea. Why put others through what I had gone through— hours of hitting balls on the ball machine just to groove a stroke, endless drills to fix patterns and court maneuvers, hours of no fun?) So I began teaching "my way." With it, women who were not particularly athletic found they could hit the ball with pace and win points by their own efforts rather than by opponents' mistakes. Women who were athletic found they could hit the ball harder with less effort, thereby increasing their ability to win. They all liked the feeling of moving freely on the court, found it similar to dance, but dance with impressive results! Men showed the most dramatic changes in their games when they finally learned to re-lax enough to allow the racket head to do the work for them—to give them endless power to hit the ball wherever they wanted. Children happily learned to play this way automatically since most of them did not have the strength to muscle the ball anyway.

I myself continued to marvel at the secrets of using this new power as I taught and played. In fact, since I was playing so well and enjoying the game so much, I decided to go back on the circuit—eventually playing the Virginia Slims Circuit and winning the 35 Women's at Forest Hills. Wherever I played, people were amazed at *how* I played. It looked different. It *was* different. They could not believe I could hit the ball so hard and be so relaxed and win as often as I did at the "advanced" age of thirty-five!

They wanted to know the secret of my power. The secret was so simple it stunned them. Read on and I'll share it with you.

Consider me your private tennis pro, and as you read this book I will show you the secrets that will win and individualize your game and style. The secrets are simple exercises that put the emphasis on the *head* of your racket, its natural movement, and your body's natural follow-through.

These exercises will be especially helpful to those who can already play the game a little, and the results will be immediate and dramatic. By learning these movements in their purest form, you will easily develop the important qualities for a winning style—relaxation, freedom, and natural power from *head-emphasis.*

First, find a comfortable chair, put up your feet if you like, and let's get acquainted. Read straight through your private lesson book and see in advance what your new coach will ask you to do. Afterward, *do exactly as instructed,* and be sure to actually *do* the exercises and experience the *feel* of them. Then, get ready to use your *head*— and win! Let's begin.

The Stance that Fits You to a T

Put your racket down. Find a good place where you can be alone and have room to move. Stand up straight. Shut your eyes. Extend your arms to either side. Your body will form the letter T. Now slowly begin to swing your arms back and forth on one level plane at shoulder height.

Turn so that your whole body will end up spinning on one toe then the other as you swing back and forth. Make sure you are spinning on a straight perpendicular axis and are not swaying from side to side as you turn. Repeat until you feel yourself in perfect balance as you move.

As you swing, be very relaxed and free. Let your head be a part of the movement. Feel the turn on your toe and your heel rising. Feel the hanging sensation at the end of each phase before going in the other direction . . . and feel the floating of your arms through the air as they swing around.

If during any part of this movement you feel tightness or tension in any part of your body, shake it out. Kick your feet. Wobble your head. Wiggle your shoulders. Move your lips. Get loose.

Notice during this exercise how freely and easily your arms move. When they are in motion, it is not necessary to hold them up or out. The force of the motion does this. In other words, once you start this motion of swinging, your whole body floats right along.

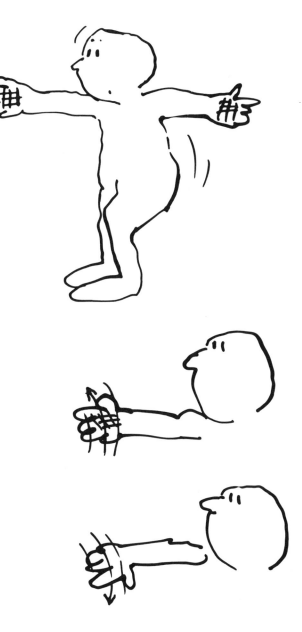

Now there is one thing more you should know about when you swing your arms: Your hands are the same as the racket face, and as they go, so goes the ball. If your hand is open (tilted back), the ball is likely to fly upward. If it is closed, you will probably top-spin the ball too much and hit it into the net.

Later you might try opening and closing the face of the racket. But for now your hand, and therefore the racket face, should be fairly straight up and down—perpendicular to the ground—when you swing. Try it.

Now try something else. Tighten your body all over and go through the same motion. You can't! You can go through the same space mechanically by turning your body, but you can't "swing" through it. This difference is very important because the *swing* is the most important element to perfect in tennis. It is the essence of your forehand, backhand, and serve.

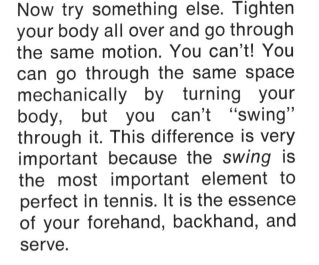

The Pendulum Swing

Okay, now try this. Relax and swing your arms in a pendulum motion, up and down. Starting at the top, eyes closed, let them fall and swing up. Again, let your whole body participate. Swing your arms up and down. Hang, fall, hang, fall. Feel the similarities to the other swing.

Now tighten and do it mechanically. Ugh! The life is gone. When you tighten, you cut off the flow of energy. Let go and feel the difference.

The Corkscrew Coil

Go stand in front of a full-length mirror. This is one movement you should *see* and feel. Put your arms straight out again and swing. Notice the twist in your body. As you turn to one side, your arms are turned in that direction more than any other part of your body, and the degree of twist diminishes as it goes down your body because your feet are fairly stationary. It's like a corkscrew.

Now turn sideways by taking a step instead of twirling. There is no twist in the torso, no coil, no torque. And it is this twist or coil that is needed to give you the force to go in the other direction and swing the racket freely, easily, and *powerfully,* without work.

Face the mirror again and watch and feel this coiling and uncoiling as you swing. You will understand this better when you put a racket in your hand later on.

Swinging— Centrifugally Speaking

Get an old long-sleeved sweatshirt, tennis sweater, or pullover and tie one arm around the body of it so that you have a nice knot at one end. Now take the free arm of the sweater in one hand, put out your arms, and swing. Swing openly and evenly. You and the sweater must swing together.

Feel the weight of the knot on the very outside of the circle as you swing, and feel the centrifugal force created by this weight being swung from a central point—your spinning axis. *This is the force that is going to hit the ball.*

Continue swinging. Feel how the weight of the knot falls when you reach one side of your swing. Let the knot rest in your other hand on the backhand side until the motion uncoils enough to send it flying back through the air in the other direction. Naturally, on the forehand side the knot will simply hang.

Now tighten your arms and swing stiffly. Notice how your arms have a different quality from the sweater. They are stiff and un-bendable. They are no longer re-laxed and flowing, and as a result the sweater jerks and flops when you swing them.

AAAAH!

Let go again and swing naturally. When relaxed, your arms move with the same fluidity as the arm of the sweater—not a bone in them. Your arms are free-swinging, smooth, and graceful. In this way the energy flows out of the center of you, down your arm, down the sweater arm (soon to be the "racket arm") to the knot (the racket head), and eventually into the ball, which takes it to the other side of the court. It is really a lining up of all of your bodily forces (including the sweater or racket) into a cohesive whole and then directing this energy clearly and cleanly down the path of the oncoming ball toward the spot *where you want the ball to go.*

Now swing the sweater all over—over your head and down around your feet. Swing it wide and away from you. Swing it so that it expands the thrust of your whole arm. Play with it—up, around, and down.

Relax and let it hang. Notice when you do this that the line of your arm and the line of the sweater arm are the same. This is how it should be when you hold the racket—so that the racket and your arm are *one.*

Now we'll try the real thing.

Hold the racket with your non-playing hand and put your playing hand open and flat against the strings of the racket head. This circular area of the racket is called the "head" of the racket, and it is what we will be most concerned with. Get to know it. Now gently slide your hand back toward the handle until the end of the racket is *well* within the heel of your hand. Then *gently* grip it—very gently—and let your arm fall.

Let it swing back and forth. Now swing it circularly, just as you did the sweater. Make sure you swing with the same quality as you did the sweater—freely and effortlessly.

Don't think in terms of tennis "strokes." This is a "swinging and throwing" motion and nothing more.

Try to treat the racket exactly as if it were the sweater, and it will take on the freedom of the sweater. It will no longer be stiff and board-like. When you have recaptured the "sweater feeling," lower your arms to about waist level, *bend* your elbows—don't lock them—and hold them somewhat away from your sides. Now swing! Let your arms fly by themselves.

Always the Center of Your Circle

Take a string about 30 feet long and make a circle around your-self. (A chalk line will do as well.) Make a line through the middle of the circle. Stand in the middle and swing with your racket. Notice that when you swing the racket back to your right, you've swung the racket open for a *forehand*—there!

30

—and when you swing it to the left, you're ready for a *backhand.* That's how you prepare for a shot on either side. You *swing* the racket open! But be sure to prepare for it early. You can't be too early. Get it back and wait around with it back. Run around with it back. But get it *back.*

As you do this on the backhand side, let the weight of the racket head rest in your left hand by gently grasping the racket's throat. Study the grip. You *do* need another grip for the backhand.

Stand facing an imaginary net and hold the racket out in front of you with the forehand grip—a very loose one. Notice as you swing to the left with your racket resting in your left hand, your right hand just slides up on top of the racket, slipping right into the backhand grip —the first finger's big knuckle is directly on top of the racket as it is held perpendicular to the ground.

Try it.

Make sure as you hold the racket in this position that you do not create an angle at the hand-and-racket connection by holding the racket head up. An angle at this connection will put the emphasis in your hand and not in the racket head where you want it to be. Your hand is only a connector between your arm and the racket, not a control center. Relax the hand and let the head drop to feel its weight. Now swing it back and let the hand slide up to the backhand grip and the weight of the head rest in the left hand.

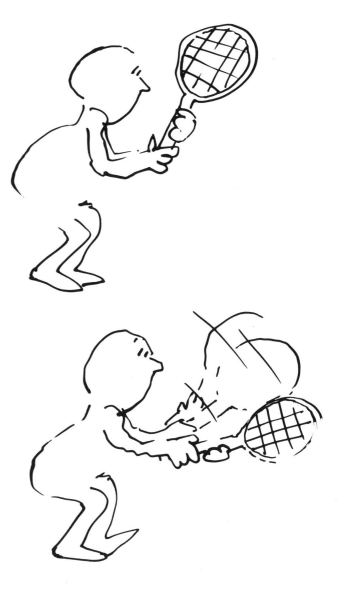

Again, *this* is the place to be, with the racket back—steady, ready to fire.

You may be wondering what the line dividing the circle is for. Stand over it so that it is between your feet—the imaginary net is in front of you and the fence is behind. Okay, there is one factor in swinging to remember—*how far back to swing.* It is critical, because the farther you swing back, the less time and more difficulty you will have in getting the racket back out in front of your body on the forward throw. Naturally, hitting the ball as far in front of you as possible in a controlled manner is of utmost importance in tennis. You can direct the ball more accurately, hit the ball faster because more of your energies will be in line with the ball, and hit it earlier, which makes it more difficult for your opponent to get to and return it. So hitting in front of you, and swinging back not too far, is very important.

Now swing.

There, that's as far as you need to go—not even halfway back. In order to do this easily, it is helpful to hold the racket well in front of you when you start. The racket has a certain distance it likes to move, so if you start with your arms away from your body in front, then swing, it is content to go only that far back. Do it on the backhand side, and make sure to hold your arms and the racket away from your body when you swing back. It allows the arm and racket to unfold smoothly and completely on the forward throw. Try it.

Now you have half of two strokes —the swing back for both the forehand and the backhand. The rest is all uphill—literally! For from this "back" spot you simply throw the racket head out and slightly up. But first, put down your racket and get an old pair of jeans or slacks.

Throwing Your Head Away

It is probably best to do this exercise outside. Knot one leg around the body of the pants—make it heavy. It's for this weight and length that we use the pants instead of the sweater this time. Now grab the long end and swing it back. Take a step forward with your left foot and with a heave-ho give it a throw—and let go. (In tennis a swing and a throw are all you need to know.)

Now do it again, and pay attention that you have your arms well away from your body so that the centrifugal force created by your throw uncoils and extends your arm and body completely. The weight of the knot when thrown pulls your body out in the direction of the throw—*it* leads *you.*

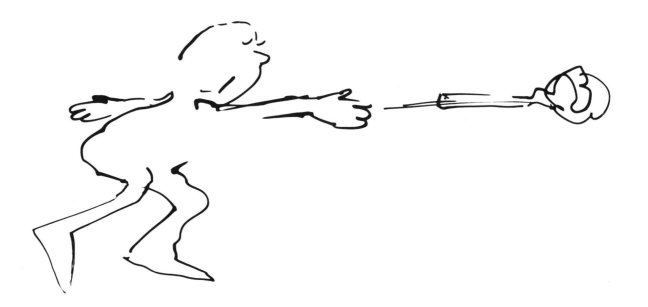

Now try it another way. Lead with your hand, then with your wrist. Try leading with your elbow, your shoulder, and then your hip, as some people do when they play tennis. It just doesn't work. When you do it right, you throw it. It pulls you. Very simple! But remember what you are throwing—the knot or weight that soon will be the head of your tennis racket—not the whole racket, but the *head*!

Try a few on your backhand side.

On this side, step in with your right foot. Notice how your body ends up leaning forward—it is being pulled that way by the throw instead of being pushed by you. As you throw, be sure you throw for distance, as if you were throwing the knot (and soon racket head) to the other end of the court. This is not a mere toss or fling but a *Throooow* . . .

Remember to always use your other arm as ballast. The arms work together as one unit—not in a fixed or stiff way, but they should open together, then twirl or spin together as the weight is thrown.

THROOOOW. . . .

This is *very* important. You are learning how to play balanced, harmonious, effortless tennis, and it requires the participation of your whole body, not just your right arm. You spin from your middle and your arms fly—and all will go well.

Really Letting Go

Now you are ready . . . to toss your *racket!*

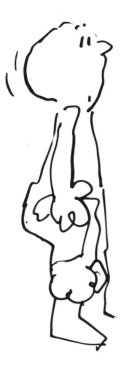

The idea of throwing for distance is important so try throwing it on a wide expanse of lawn. Hold the racket loosely and swing back, letting the head hang.

Step and T H R O W . . .

Throw and . . . let go.

Try again—still stretched out, in perfect balance, weight forward. Try a few more on both sides. Try high ones and low ones. All with the same formula—swing back, racket head hanging, and throw.

Swing high and throw . . . and low and throw.

Did you feel it? Perfect forehands and backhands every time!

And so you have found the second half of both the forehand and backhand— the throw.

You are now ready to try it with the ball. You may have to use a ball machine. Even better, get a kind friend who will hit the ball easily enough to you so you can get the feel of swinging and throwing with the ball. But take a break now and let your lesson "sink in." Then try it with the ball.

Swinging and Throwing and Finger Hinging

Be sure when you do this that you don't alter what you've already learned to do. Stay with the continuous flowing motion and feeling, letting the racket head do the work. Remember, "swing and throw—that's all you do, you know!"

Try it . . . .

AAAAH!

Perfect! And a good "aaah" always helps.

50

OOOOH!

Continue. Better? Be sure to allow the head of the racket to make its full arc as it unfolds and extends your arm. In fact, here is a little exercise to help you really feel this arc in its purest form. Try it on the backhand side first. We'll call it "finger hinging." Hold the racket with your thumb on top of the racket butt and index finger underneath to create a hinge. Use the other fingers, and the first finger of the left hand under the throat of the racket, for support.

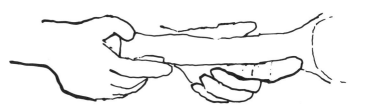

51

Now swing back easily and let it go. See how the head makes a semicircle or arc as the whole arm unfolds. Stand a little behind the service line and try it with the ball —very easily, or you'll lose the racket. Be sure you feel the movement of the racket *in* your hand as it hinges between the fingers. This is very important, because when you hold the racket with the proper grip you must allow this same movement to occur *within* your hand.

Try the same thing on the forehand side, holding the racket between your fingers. It is a little more difficult because there is no other hand to rest the racket head on. So just do it gently . . . That's it. Now hold the racket with the regular forehand grip, grip it tightly, and swing. The hinge occurs in the wrist here, instead of within the hand.

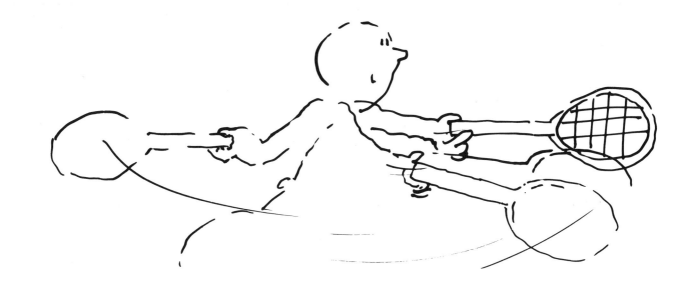

Hold the racket without any tension and swing freely, again feeling the movement of the racket *within* the hand. Naturally, the wrist hinges, but as a part of the unfolding of the whole arm. This hinging within the hand is essential to the freedom of the movement and must be retained no matter how hard you end up hitting the ball. So be aware of it.

The Meeting Place

Okay, now comes the question of when and where to meet the ball. The answer is as soon as you can, and as far out in front of you as possible—without straining or hurrying, of course. This means the swing back must be early. Even before you know for sure which way the ball is coming, start the racket moving, and then wait with it back.

Take a moment here to consider the ball in a new way—as very light, even weightless, no longer a solid object but a long, endless flow of energy that glides back and forth across the net. And all you have to do with the racket back is line the head up with this flow, step forward, and throw—*flow* into it, and direct that flow of energy where you want it to go. There is no real "hit" or point of contact or impact—merely a flowing in and out of this line of energy.

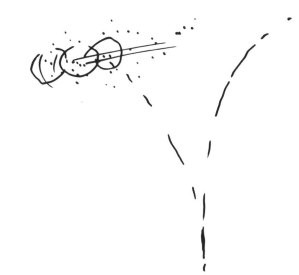

When mastered, *this removes once and for all any possibility of developing a tennis elbow.* It also makes the motion, with or without the ball, look the same—smooth and even, without a hitch or "hit" to it.

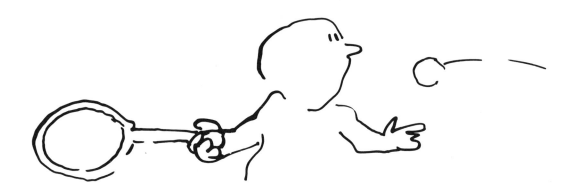

A way to confirm that you are doing this successfully is to swing at a ball or two with a racket without any strings. When you swing this racket and you make a great effort or lurch at the ball as it passes through the racket, you are paying attention to the *ball* and not to the *motion.* Make sure you swing the same whether there is a ball there or not—smooth and even. You must stay so relaxed, and hold the racket so loosely, that *you* are able to flow into *that* stream of energy.

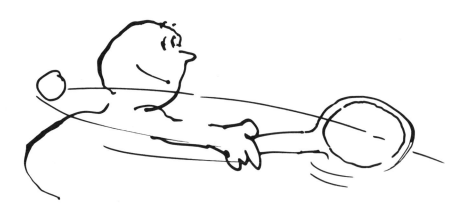

The Earlier the Better

And now, specifically, when to throw?

E A R L Y ! !

The farther in front of you you meet the ball, the more extended you are and the more lined up your energies will be. It feels better and works better. Experiment with this. Remember, you cannot meet the ball too far in front of you. Try it on the backhand side. Step, throw, flow.

Except for beginners, players often insist that the backhand is a much easier and more natural stroke than the forehand. It's easy to see why. The shoulder of the racket arm is already out in front of your spinning axis on the backhand side. It is closer to the oncoming ball, and when the arm is unfolded, the arm, hand, and racket are well out in front of this axis when you meet the ball. On the forehand side, however, the shoulder, arm, hand, and racket are *behind* the axis, and many people never get it out, so they wind up hitting the ball late and across their bodies.

Oooott!

This should be no problem for you, since you already know how to twirl your arms as you throw so that the right shoulder gets out in front and you can easily meet the ball way out there. It is imperative, though, to start early and leave yourself plenty of room between you and the ball to do this. Remember that as you move, so does your axis. So if you are moving forward to a short ball, leave yourself plenty of room to twirl and not overrun the ball. It is the relationship between the *racket head and the ball* that you must get a sense of, not your own head and the ball.

As you continue swinging and throwing, be sure you step forward with the proper foot—the foot opposite the side you are swinging on. Step slightly toward that side on a diagonal and let your weight move out on it. This, of course, is "cross-stepping." Practice this on both sides.

Taking Aim and Firing

While you rally, you should know how to direct the ball. Very simple —you just throw the head of the racket where you want the ball to go—and let go. Don't let go of the racket, of course, but let go of the control. Allow the head to hang onto the ball and guide it to that spot.

You may also want to know about top spin—not exaggerated top spin, but the top spin that keeps the ball in the court on a put-away drive or simple rally. It is nothing to worry about. It happens automatically when the racket is left relaxed. By just uncoiling on your throw forward, you should be moving on a slight upward spiral, and this will do it easily. Watch the fall of the ball and always be below the ball when you begin to uncoil. This is true for high balls, low balls, and everything in between. The spin is automatic, so be at ease. Feel it uncoil?

Now, if you want to do something like a lob, you merely throw the racket head up the line you want the ball to travel and, again, let go. If you stop the head, you will pop the ball and make it flop. So be sure to let the motion go when you throw. This will put the proper spin on the ball to keep it in.

For Speed's Sake

As for power and speed, these come on their own, and they come better when you are relaxed and free-swinging. So there is no need to push it. Let it happen naturally. It is far better to play in harmony— in a rhythm that is comfortable for you—than to strain. Real progress is never achieved except from this simple point of self-harmony and balance. If you remain on this point, you will improve steadily and soundly, even if you are not aware of it.

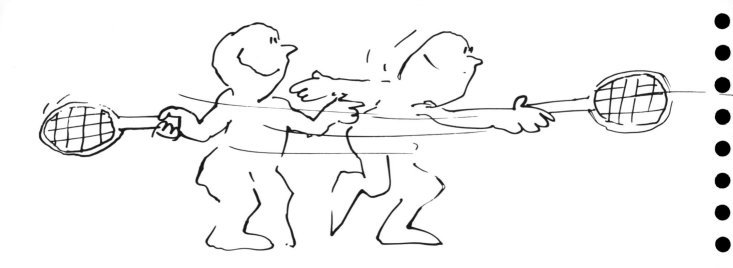

Before we move on, try a few shots—and really whack 'em. Just throw the racket full out and see what happens. Isn't that great?

Now go back to the place where you can comfortably keep a rally going, and practice the purity of the movement, the lining up with the ball, and the going with the flow.

ZOOOM !

Even if your form and strokes are well established, you may enjoy doing what you already do with a little different emphasis. "Swing" the racket open. The line of the swing is not so important as the *quality* of swinging. It gives you the life. Do this early and wait— *"hang"*—then *throw* the racket head freely out and let it pull the racket, arm, and body forward. Of course, you must hold the racket loosely in order to do this. You can't throw and hold on at the same time.

Watch for magical results!

Session 3   The Serve Is Up to U

Okay, put your racket and the balls down and stand behind the baseline, perpendicular to it. Your left foot should be pointing to the right at a slight angle. Your right foot is behind it and parallel to the line. Now face sideways, put your arms together and in front of you toward the net, and let them drop. Your left hand touches your left leg and comes up. Your right hand swings by your belly and comes up. Swing them up and down together as if you were leading a band. Swing them high and even —but be sure to *swing* them. Stop once at the top and see how high they are. Check that they form a U and are together. Make sure they swing down together and up together.

Now try this with the racket. Hold it between the backhand and forehand grips, but hold only the end of the racket so it can wing around when you swing it. Make sure your feet are lined up, square off the shoulders, arms high and in front of you. Now let 'em go! Notice at the very bottom how your hand and the racket flip over—open up —and then swing up with an open face.

Up at the top of the U, let the racket head drop behind your head. But *don't drop your elbow!* It will put your shoulders at an angle, and you'll never get the racket back up without a lot of unnecessary work. Instead, keep your elbow high and your shoulders level, and drop only the top part of your arm.

From there, throw the racket head high into the air and let it fall across your body, past your left leg.

Naturally, you'll feel the weight change on your feet from the throw forward, but there's no need to walk your feet around just yet.

Try it again, and when you get to the top make the drop and throw of the racket a kind of continuous loop. Be sure this is high in the sky. Repeat this several times.

69

Figure Eights

Now that you've got the line of the motion, let's work on the quality. Put the racket down and go get that old sweatshirt or sweater with the knot in it we used in Session 1 and assume the same position.

Go!

OH!

That's the point. You must swing this substitute racket as you did before on the ground strokes, using the centrifigual force created by swinging the weighty head. Try it again. Swing it away from you and let the swing take *you*.

Feel it? Now swing it continuously like a figure eight. Keep it going. Feel the natural rhythm the swing makes. It hangs at the top like all swings that pause at one point before going or falling in the other direction.

Tossing without Turning

Now you're ready for the real thing.

Take the racket and a ball in your left hand. Try it. But don't forget to let go! When you swing your hand up for the toss, you simply open your hand and let the ball go. It should be right where you want it. But it will take a little practice.

The key is to swing the ball arm all the way down to your leg and straight back up. Do this cleanly without letting it turn or wander around on the trip, and the ball should be in just the right spot. The right spot in height is nice and high in the air so that your right arm and the racket are almost fully extended when the racket meets the ball. The right spot in relation to your body, forward and backward, is a few inches in front of your left foot when you let the ball drop to the court.

The Finger Hinge—on the Serve

Try a few serves, but be sure you hold the racket loosely so that you get the same quality as in swinging the sweater. Here is a little secret to help you let the racket move more freely on the serve: Hold it with the same grip, but hold it with only two fingers—the thumb on one side of the racket and the index finger on the other side. Let the other fingers just help out a little. Now allow the racket to hinge in these fingers, as you did in the exercise for the ground strokes. Do it gently at first or you'll put a hole in the court if you drop the racket! You can sense how much you have to hang onto the racket. But the secret is to allow it to hinge *between* the fingers.

See? You've got the line to follow, the quality of swinging, the hanging and falling. Now just hit a lot of balls, and when you're doing it, occasionally smack a few—just to show what a powerful serve you are going to have when it all comes together.

Later, when you have the motion down, you may want to experiment a little. Try serving with the grip farther toward the backhand for more spin. While doing this, keep the toss high and toward you. Also try the grip more toward the forehand side for a flatter serve. Throw the ball a bit lower and more in front of you. Do all this slowly to begin with, and always freely and easily.

Session 4

Out of the Frying Pan

I'm not joking. Go get a frying pan and come to the net. Nothing in cast iron. Something light and simple. A 10-inch pan is preferable, but an 8-inch one will do.

If you can, have a friend hit you a few easy balls. You just pop them back, right from the inside of the ol' frying pan. This is what most beginners and eternal novices do —they *pop* the ball. The hand cocks back at the wrist, then snaps forward—tip tap, pit pat, POP. This may be fine for them, but not good enough for a future world-class competitor or even a good social player. You need a more dramatic shot—a chop! Not back and forth, but up and down and a little around.

Face the net a good arm and pan's length away. Put your arms out in front. Lift the pan up on a diagonal by *cocking* your wrist and swinging your forearm up a bit—but keep your arm well in front of you. The face of the pan should be held on the same diagonal as the diagonal plane you are moving on. When the ball comes, step forward and *chop* by moving the head of the frying pan back down that diagonal plane. Chop!

On lower balls that fall below the level of the net, you may need to cup the ball a little to get them back across. Sort of caress the back of the ball—like a comma in shape. This is why the pan is so good. It gives you a sense of this slight roundness to the movement. The effects will be more dramatic with the racket because the strings tend to grab the ball, backspin it, and undercut it slightly.

This is an area you can experiment with—in the degree of roundness to the chop and the amount of "umph" you put on the ball. It will give you a great variety of shots, from little drop volleys to line drive volleys. Try a few more . . . and some on the backhand, which is just the same. Turn the pan so that the face is open to the ball, and support it with your left hand. Cock your wrist by lifting the head. Chop! This cocking motion at the wrist is the secret to the volley. Without it, forget it. So practice it!

Keeping your arms out in front and letting this entire movement happen in front of your body is very important. It is much easier to see the ball and to move the pan or racket out there. Also, you won't get hit on the nose if a ball comes down the middle.

Karate Chopping

Try the real racket. Make the volleys crisp. Stop as soon as you hit the ball, like a karate chop—step and hit at the same time. For added emphasis, shout the word "hut" as you make contact with the ball. It concentrates your energy and catapults it forward as you pounce on the ball. "Hut!" (This is useful in practice but might be disturbing to your opponent and therefore unethical in match play!) You may also find it helpful in the beginning to "choke up a little" on the racket for better control. Try it.

HUT!

As you stand up there chopping and "hutting," consider your feet. Move out on a V by stepping out and across to hit the ball. *Never* let the ball come to you. Go after *it*! Go!

Have this same sense of moving on a V in the backcourt or wherever you are on the court. That way you will always be stepping in, going after it. Scoot around and position yourself to the ball so you can make this happen.

Try some lower volleys. You may have to open the face of the racket a little more. As you do, be sure you are moving the racket on the same line as the tilt of the face, and curve it under the ball a little as you move the racket forward. Also, bend your knees.

For higher volleys, close the face a little—but be sure to keep it open slightly. This will put a little backspin on the ball as you chop it and help keep it in the court if you give it some added speed or pace. As you reach higher for shots, you are moving into the field of the overhead.

Smashing

This is nothing but an abbreviated serve—without the toss-up or windup. Just hold the racket up, then let it fall behind your head. When the ball looks like it is in the right spot, throw the racket head through it. Keep the other arm up for balance.

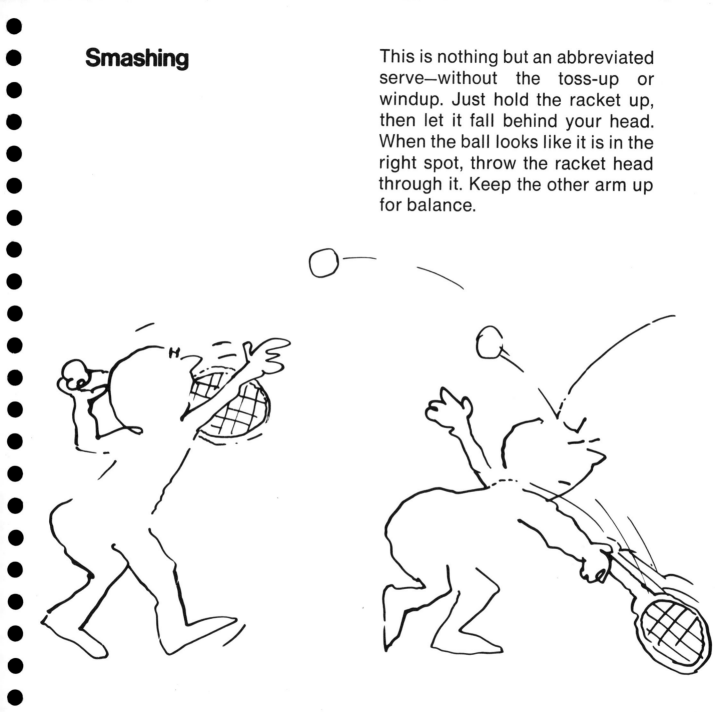

Don't worry if you miss some. Please remember it is very important to miss the ball a few times. It is the only way to know where the right spot is. Do it again, and this time very slowly and gently. This just takes a little practice, as does everything in tennis, but it's this kind of practice that *always* pays off.

Now you know how to hit anything off the ground with your swinging and throwing forehands and backhands, anything at the net with chops and "huts," and anything in the air with your overhead. You also know how to start things off with a devastating serve.

Congratulations!

Any of these skills, of course, can be altered to meet the situation or inspiration:

• Chops may be used in the backcourt.
• Chops may be turned into slices by lengthening them.
• Volleys may be pops as well as chops when the need calls.

Practice! Experiment! And *individualize* your game. Develop your own natural power with a good, easy style.

There are still a few more tips you might find of interest—the really good stuff! But take a break now. You deserve it.

Playing for the Fun of It

These tips will help you to find mental freedom on the court. You have seen how important it is to play the game with physical freedom—relaxed and easy. It is equally important to play with mental and emotional freedom. This means playing without inner tension—tension created perhaps by your own "advice" or criticism ("I shouldn't have done that." "Why didn't I remember to do that?"). Or tension created by overcompetitive demands ("I hit a good shot! I should get the point!"). Or tension created by "psyching" yourself too much: ("I gotta get this point." "Come on!" "Let's go!"). This mental pushing can ruin your game. Playing *freely* and *peacefully* inside is the way to play powerfully and really enjoy the game. Freedom to try what you like without feeling impatient with occasional unsuccessful results. Freedom from feeling resentment because you didn't win or play well.

Unless you are a professional, winning or losing a match has little to do with playing tennis. Enjoying yourself, winning *or* losing, is where the true pleasure lies. This attitude is helpful in doubles and especially mixed doubles. Learn to play without expecting anything at all of your partner. Allow him or her the freedom you must also allow yourself—that you can miss every ball that comes over the net and it's still all right. After all, it's only a game. You will be surprised at how well your partner will respond to knowing that you both share this special kind of freedom—and how well *you* will play, too.

If you are an especially competitive player, try this: Play the game as if you have no points coming to you—as if what you receive is a gift! Give your all, ask nothing in return, and see how great the reward is. (You'll be amazed!)

As far as strategy is concerned, you may sometimes find it is better to let yourself be surprised by what happens than it is to be the schemer with elaborate plans. The more diddling you do in your mind, the more you will be out of tune with the total game. Far better to be free at the right moment to hit the ball where you want to than to be preoccupied with a plan that fails to be in tune with what is really happening on the court. Tennis is a spontaneous game, a kaleidoscopic set of plays. Be ready, be free to respond.

Practice well first and do all your "thinking." Then play quickly and freely on court by instinct and inspiration, and you'll be far ahead of anyone who is out there scheming.

Once again: One of the most useful exercises in tennis is to play and *enjoy* the game and not give a hoot about the results.

Remember that tennis power comes from being relaxed and swinging the racket head freely. Enjoy yourself, and now you're on your own.

Helpful Terms

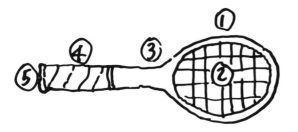

Racket: This is a tennis racket. It comes in all shapes, sizes, weights, colors, and materials, but all have the same features. These are:

1. The head—the rounded end of the racket that holds the strings.

2. The face—the stringed area. When it is tilted back, "the face is open"; when it is tipped forward, "the face is closed."

3. The throat or neck—the connecting part of the racket between the head and the handle.

4. The grip—the leather strip that covers the handle of the racket. The strip and the actual holding of the racket are called the grip.

5. The butt—the tail end of the racket. It is usually a little larger than the handle so that your grip won't slip.

Stroke: This refers to the motion a player makes with the racket to hit the ball.

Shot: This is the resulting hit of the ball after the player has made the stroke.

Forehand: This refers to the stroke as well as the resulting shot made by a right-handed player on the right side or by a left-handed player on the left.

Backhand: This, too, can be the stroke or shot a player makes. For a right-handed player the backhand is on the left side, and for a left-handed player it is on the right. In other words, the *back* of the hand faces the ball.

Serve: The serve or service can mean either the stroke or shot. The serve is normally an overhead motion, and the hitting of a serve starts play off in every point.

Volley: This is a shot hit in the air on either the forehand or backhand side. It is not high enough for a player to take a full swing, so he or she takes a short chop or punch at the ball. It is usually—and most effectively—done when the player is fairly close to the net.

Lob: This is a lofty shot usually used to go over an opponent's head when he or she is at net. It can also be used when a player is in trouble and needs time to regroup. The height of the shot gives the player this time.

Overhead smash: Sometimes referred to as an "overhead" or a "smash." This is a shot in which a player reaches high over his or her head and slams the ball across the net into the court, often for a point. It is generally the countershot to the lob.

Spin: The turning or rotating of the ball in flight. A ball may be spun in any direction. This is produced by the various angles the racket face may be in and the various directions it may be moving in as it moves across the ball.

Top spin: Here the ball spins forward in the same direction as it is being hit. Top spin makes it possible to hit a ground stroke quite hard and still keep the ball in the court. Playing

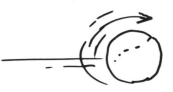

"spinny" tennis, and especially top-spin tennis, is very much in vogue now. Many of the top tournaments are being played on slower surfaces, such as clay, and hard, flat shots are less effective and more exhausting for the long matches that slower surfaces create.

Backspin: This turns the ball backward as it flies forward, so when it bounces it does not move forward toward the player, but rather stops

short and stands up. It can be tricky to handle if you are receiving such a shot unless you know what the ball is going to do.

Slice: This is the motion used to create certain spins. On forehands and backhands, the face of the racket is laid open somewhat and the head of the racket is thrown from high to low through the back of the ball. The resulting ball tends to slide or slip when it bounces—also very tricky! On a sliced serve, the face of the racket is not flat to the ball but moves across it at a diagonal—up and around—the amount depending upon the amount of spin desired. The ball comes off the ground with a nice hop. The face of the racket may slice across and around a ball in almost any direction.

Cut: This is the same as a slice, but the motion is usually short and crisp rather than long and flowing. The resulting shot stops more than on a slice.

Rally: A rally is the extended play of the ball back and forth across the net.

Cross-stepping: This refers to the stepping action a player makes as he or she is about to hit the ball. He steps forward and slightly toward the side he is hitting on—either forehand or backhand—with the opposite foot to that side. So if he is stepping to his right he steps forward and into the ball on his left foot, and vice versa.

Tie-breaker: This is a fairly new invention in tennis scoring. To prevent sets from running on into the teens (18-all, 19-all) or twenties (24-all, 28-all) and disrupt tournament scheduling or television programming, at 6-all in a set a tie-breaker is played to determine the set winner. This may be a 9-point tie-breaker, usually used in social tennis, or a 12-point tie-breaker, reserved for tournament play. In the 9-pointer, the player or team who wins 5 out of the possible 9 points wins the set, 7 games to 6. In the 12-pointer, it is the best 7 out of 12 points that wins. There is an elaborate system of who serves first and when to change courts. This varies at different courts and clubs depending on the understanding of the tie-breaker rules. It is best to simply follow the local routine and concentrate on playing the point. Let the others get lost in the logistics.

Tennis elbow: An injury in the elbow joint due to constant irritation in that area. In tennis it can be caused by the constant impact of the ball with a stiff arm or by simply swinging at the ball incorrectly, such as turning or twisting the arm unnaturally on the ground strokes. It is usually considered a type of bursitis and is very unpleasant to have and difficult to get over. Most people get a cortisone shot and hope for the best, but this is *not* the best. The only solution is to stop playing tennis until the elbow heals and then correct the motion that has created it.

"The" elbow: Also known as "choking up," this refers to a state of tension and tightened muscles, especially those of the playing arm, to the extent that the player is barely able to hit the ball over the net. This state may be created by fear of losing, fear of looking bad, even too great a desire to win, and usually occurs on crucial points, such as tie-breakers or match points, at the beginning of a match, or on the center court of Wimbledon. The solution is to play tennis for *sheer enjoyment,* without worrying about the circumstances or the outcome.

See you on the courts!

95